151 QUOTES THAT WILL IMPACT YOUR LIFE

RITIK AGARWAL

you'll find blank papers in this book, you can write thoughts which you most believe in.

Contents

Acknowledgements

Thank to all of you for your guidience.

CHAPTER ONE

151 Quotes

1. "The purpose of our lives is to be happy." — Dalai Lama

2. "Life is what happens when you're busy making other plans." — John Lennon

3. "Get busy living or get busy dying." — Stephen King

4. "You only live once, but if you do it right, once is enough." — Mae West

5. "Many of life's failures are people who did not realize how close they were to success when they gave up."– Thomas A. Edison

6. "If you want to live a happy life, tie it to a goal, not to people or things."– Albert Einstein

7. "Never let the fear of striking out keep you from playing the game."– Babe Ruth

8. "Money and success don't change people; they merely amplify what is already there." — Will Smith

9. "Your time is limited, so don't waste it living someone else's life. Don't be trapped by dogma – which is living with the results of other people's thinking." – Steve Jobs

10. "Not how long, but how well you have lived is the main thing." — Seneca

11. "If life were predictable it would cease to be life, and be without flavor." – Eleanor Roosevelt

12. "The whole secret of a successful life is to find out what is one's destiny to do, and then do it."– Henry Ford

13. "In order to write about life first you must live it."– Ernest Hemingway

14. "The big lesson in life, baby, is never be scared of anyone or anything."– Frank Sinatra

15. "Sing like no one's listening, love like you've never been hurt, dance like nobody's watching, and live like it's heaven on earth." –

16. "Curiosity about life in all of its aspects, I think, is still the secret of great creative people." – Leo Burnett

17. "Life is not a problem to be solved, but a reality to be experienced."– Soren Kierkegaard

18. "The unexamined life is not worth living." — Socrates

19. "Turn your wounds into wisdom." — Oprah Winfrey

20. "The way I see it, if you want the rainbow, you gotta put up with the rain." —Dolly Parton

21. "Do all the good you can, for all the people you can, in all the ways you can, as long as you can." — Hillary Clinton (inspired by John Wesley quote)

22. "Don't settle for what life gives you; make life better and build something." — Ashton Kutcher

23. "Everybody wants to be famous, but nobody wants to do the work. I live by that. You grind hard so you can play hard. At the end of the day, you put all the work in, and eventually it'll pay off. It could be in a year, it could be in 30 years. Eventually, your hard work will pay off." — Kevin Hart

24. "Everything negative – pressure, challenges – is all an opportunity for me to rise." — Kobe Bryant

25. "I like criticism. It makes you strong." — LeBron James

26. "You never really learn much from hearing yourself speak." — George Clooney

27. "Life imposes things on you that you can't control, but you still have the choice of how you're going to live through this." — Celine Dion

28. "Life is never easy. There is work to be done and obligations to be met – obligations to truth, to justice, and to liberty." —

29. "Live for each second without hesitation." — Elton John

30. "Life is like riding a bicycle. To keep your balance, you must keep moving." — Albert Einstein

31. "Life is really simple, but men insist on making it complicated." — Confucius

32. "Life is a succession of lessons which must be lived to be understood." — Helen Keller

33. "Your work is going to fill a large part of your life, and the only way to be truly satisfied is to do what you believe is great work. And the only way to do great work is to love what you do. If you haven't found it yet, keep looking. Don't settle. As with all matters of the heart, you'll know when you find it." — Steve Jobs

34. "My mama always said, life is like a box of chocolates. You never know what you're gonna get." — Forrest Gump (<u>Forrest Gump Quotes</u>)

35. "Watch your thoughts; they become words. Watch your words; they become actions. Watch your actions; they become habits. Watch your habits; they become character. Watch your character; it becomes your destiny."— Lao-Tze

36. "When we do the best we can, we never know what miracle is wrought in our life or the life of another." — Helen Keller

37. "The healthiest response to life is joy." — Deepak Chopra

38. "Life is like a coin. You can spend it any way you wish, but you only spend it once." — Lillian Dickson

39. "The best portion of a good man's life is his little nameless, unencumbered acts of kindness and of love." — Wordsworth

40. "In three words I can sum up everything I've learned about life: It goes on." — Robert Frost

41. "Life is ten percent what happens to you and ninety percent how you respond to it." — Charles Swindoll

42. "Keep calm and carry on." — <u>Winston Churchill</u>

43. "Maybe that's what life is... a wink of the eye and winking stars." — Jack Kerouac

44. "Life is a flower of which love is the honey." — Victor Hugo

45. "Keep smiling, because life is a beautiful thing and there's so much to <u>smile</u> about." — <u>Marilyn Monroe</u>

46. "Health is the greatest gift, contentment the greatest wealth, faithfulness the best relationship." — <u>Buddha</u>

47. "You have brains in your head. You have feet in your shoes. You can steer yourself any direction you choose." — <u>Dr. Seuss</u>

48. "Good friends, good books, and a sleepy conscience: this is the ideal life." — <u>Mark Twain</u>

49. "Life would be tragic if it weren't funny." — Stephen Hawking

50. "Live in the sunshine, swim the sea, drink the wild air." — Ralph Waldo Emerson

51. "The greatest pleasure of life is love." — Euripides

52. "Life is what we make it, always has been, always will be." — Grandma Moses

53. "Life's tragedy is that we get old too soon and wise too late." — Benjamin Franklin

54. "Life is about making an impact, not making an income." — Kevin Kruse

55. "I've missed more than 9000 shots in my career. I've lost almost 300 games. 26 times I've been trusted to take the game winning shot and missed. I've failed over and over and over again in my life. And that is why I succeed." – Michael Jordan

56. "Every strike brings me closer to the next home run." – Babe Ruth

57. "The two most important days in your life are the day you are born and the day you find out why." – Mark Twain

58. "Life shrinks or expands in proportion to one's courage." – Anais Nin

59. "When I was 5 years old, my mother always told me that happiness was the key to life. When I went to school, they asked me what I wanted to be when I grew up. I wrote down 'happy'. They told me I didn't understand the assignment, and I told them they didn't understand life." – John Lennon

Related: 100 Mother's Day Quotes for Mom

60. "Too many of us are not living our dreams because we are living our fears." – Les Brown

61. "I believe every human has a finite number of heartbeats. I don't intend to waste any of mine." —Neil Armstrong

62. "Live as if you were to die tomorrow. Learn as if you were to live forever." —Mahatma Gandhi

63. "If you live long enough, you'll make mistakes. But if you learn from them, you'll be a better person." —Bill Clinton

64. "Life is short, and it is here to be lived." —Kate Winslet

65. "The longer I live, the more beautiful life becomes." —Frank Lloyd Wright

66. "Every moment is a fresh beginning." —T.S. Eliot

67. "When you cease to dream you cease to live." —Malcolm Forbes

68. "If you spend your whole life waiting for the storm, you'll never enjoy the sunshine." —Morris West

69. "Don't cry because it's over, smile because it happened." —Dr. Seuss

70. "If you can do what you do best and be happy, you're further along in life than most people." —Leonardo DiCaprio

71. "We should remember that just as a positive outlook on life can promote good health, so can everyday acts of kindness." —Hillary Clinton

72. "Don't limit yourself. Many people limit themselves to what they think they can do. You can go as far as your mind lets you. What you believe, remember, you can achieve." —Mary Kay Ash

73. "It is our choices that show what we truly are, far more than our abilities." —J. K. Rowling

74. "If you're not stubborn, you'll give up on experiments too soon. And if you're not flexible, you'll pound your head against the wall and you won't see a different solution to a problem you're trying to solve." —Jeff Bezos

75. "The best way to predict your future is to create it." — Abraham Lincoln

76. "You must expect great things of yourself before you can do them." —Michael Jordan

77. "Identity is a prison you can never escape, but the way to redeem your past is not to run from it, but to try to understand it, and use it as a foundation to grow." —Jay-Z

78. "There are no mistakes, only opportunities." —Tina Fey

79. "It takes 20 years to build a reputation and five minutes to ruin it. If you think about that, you'll do things differently." —Warren Buffett

80. "As you grow older, you will discover that you have two hands, one for helping yourself, the other for helping others." —Audrey Hepburn

81. "Sometimes you can't see yourself clearly until you see yourself through the eyes of others." —Ellen DeGeneres

82. "You must not lose faith in humanity. Humanity is an ocean; if a few drops of the ocean are dirty, the ocean does not become dirty." —Mahatma Gandhi

83. "All life is an experiment. The more experiments you make, the better." – Ralph Waldo Emerson

84. "Here's to the crazy ones, the misfits, the rebels, the troublemakers, the round pegs in the square holes ... the ones who see things differently — they're not fond of rules ... You can quote them, disagree with them, glorify or vilify them, but the only thing you can't do is ignore them because they change things ... They push the human race forward, and while some may see them as the crazy ones, we see genius ..." – Steve Jobs

85. "It had long since come to my attention that people of accomplishment rarely sat back and let things happen to them. They went out and happened to things." – Leonardo Da Vinci

86. "Throughout life people will make you mad, disrespect you and treat you bad. Let God deal with the things they do, cause hate in your heart will consume you too." — Will Smith

87. "Do not dwell in the past, do not dream of the future, concentrate the mind on the present moment."– *Buddha*

88. "Life is a dream for the wise, a game for the fool, a comedy for the rich, a tragedy for the poor." – Sholom Aleichem

89. "If you love life, don't waste time, for time is what life is made up of." – Bruce Lee

90. When one door closes, another opens; but we often look so long and so regretfully upon the closed door that we do not see the one that has opened for us. – Alexander Graham Bell

91. "Never take life seriously. Nobody gets out alive anyway." — Anonymous

92. "Be happy for this moment. This moment is your life." – Omar Khayyam

93. "Happiness is the feeling that power increases — that resistance is being overcome." — Friedrich Nietzsche

94. "I have learned to seek my happiness by limiting my desires, rather than in attempting to satisfy them." — John Stuart Mill

95. "The secret of happiness, you see is not found in seeking more, but in developing the capacity to enjoy less."-Socrates

96. "The more man meditates upon good thoughts, the better will be his world and the world at large." — Confucius

97. "The greatest blessings of mankind are within us and within our reach. A wise man is content with his lot, whatever it may be, without wishing for what he has not."— Seneca

98. "Happiness is like a butterfly; the more you chase it, the more it will elude you, but if you turn your attention to other things, it will come and sit softly on your shoulder." — Henry David Thoreau

99. "When it is obvious that goals can't be reached, don't adjust the goals, but adjust the action steps." — Confucius

100. "There may be people who have more talent than you, but there's no excuse for anyone to work harder than you do – and I believe that." — Derek Jeter

101. "Don't be afraid to fail. It's not the end of the world, and in many ways, it's the first step toward learning something and getting better at it." — Jon Hamm

102. "Life is very interesting... in the end, some of your greatest pains, become your greatest strengths." – Drew Barrymore

103. "I think if you live in a black-and-white world, you're gonna suffer a lot. I used to be like that. But I don't believe that anymore." – Bradley Cooper

104. "I don't believe in happy endings, but I do believe in happy travels, because ultimately, you die at a very young age, or you live long enough to watch your friends die. It's a mean thing, life." – George Clooney

105. "It's never too late – never too late to start over, never too late to be happy." – <u>Jane Fonda</u>

106. "You're only human. You live once and life is wonderful, so eat the damned red velvet cupcake." – Emma Stone

107. "A lot of people give up just before they're about to make it. You know you never know when that next obstacle is going to be the last one." – <u>Chuck Norris</u> (related: 101 <u>Chuck Norris Jokes</u>)

108. "Be nice to people on the way up, because you may meet them on the way down." – Jimmy Durante

109. "I believe you make your day. You make your life. So much of it is all perception, and this is the form that I built for myself. I have to accept it and work within those compounds, and it's up to me." – Brad Pitt

110. "The minute that you're not learning I believe you're dead." – Jack Nicholson

111. "Life's tough, but it's tougher when you're stupid." – John Wayne

112. "Take up one idea. Make that one idea your life -- think of it, dream of it, live on that idea. Let the brain, muscles, nerves, every part of your body be full of that idea, and just leave every other idea alone. This is the way to success." — Swami Vivekananda

113. "I guess it comes down to a simple choice, really. Get busy living or get busy dying." — *Shawshank Redemption*

114. "When we strive to become better than we are, everything around us becomes better too." — Paulo Coelho

115. "There are three things you can do with your life: You can waste it, you can spend it, or you can invest it. The best use of your life is to invest it in something that will last longer than your time on Earth." — Rick Warren

116. "You only pass through this life once, you don't come back for an encore." — Elvis Presley

117. "In the long run, the sharpest weapon of all is a kind and gentle spirit." — Anne Frank

118. "You're not defined by your past; you're prepared by it. You're stronger, more experienced, and you have greater <u>confidence</u>." — Joel Osteen

119. "We become not a melting pot but a beautiful mosaic. Different people, different beliefs, different yearnings, different hopes, different

dreams." — Jimmy Carter

120. "Nothing is more honorable than a grateful heart." — Seneca

121. "Once you figure out who you are and what you love about yourself, I think it all kinda falls into place." — Jennifer Aniston

122. "Happy is the man who can make a living by his hobby." — George Bernard Shaw

123. "Just disconnect. Once in a day sometime, sit silently and from all connections disconnect yourself." — Yoda (Star Wars Quotes)

124. "Be where you are; otherwise you will miss your life." — Buddha

125. "Living an experience, a particular fate, is accepting it fully." — Albert Camus

126. "The more you praise and celebrate your life, the more there is in life to celebrate." — Oprah Winfrey

127. "Your image isn't your character. Character is what you are as a person." — Derek Jeter

128. "Football is like life, it requires perseverance, self-denial, hard work sacrifice, dedication and respect for authority." —Vince Lombardi

129. "As you know, life is an echo; we get what we give." — David DeNotaris

130. "There are no regrets in life, just lessons."   Jennifer Aniston

131. "I believe that nothing in life is unimportant every moment can be a beginning." — John McLeod

132. "Find people who will make you better." — Michelle Obama

133. "As my knowledge of things grew I felt more and more the delight of the world I was in." — Helen Keller

134. "Benjamin Franklin was a humanitarian that dedicated his life to making contributions to all humans. He had a clear purpose for himself: improve the human race." — Paulo Braga

135. "You cannot control everything that happens to you; you can only control the way you respond to what happens. In your response is your power." — Anonymous

136. "Don't allow your past or present condition to control you. It's just a process that you're going through to get you to the next level." – T.D. Jakes

137. "You will meet two kinds of people in life: ones who build you up and ones who tear you down. But in the end, you'll thank them both." — Anonymous

138. "My mission in life is not merely to survive, but to thrive; and to do so with some passion, some compassion, some humor, and some style." –

<u>Maya Angelou</u>

139. "If we don't change, we don't grow. If we don't grow, we aren't really living." – Gail Sheehy

140. "You choose the life you live. If you don't like it, it's on you to change it because no one else is going to do it for you." – Kim Kiyosaki

141. "It is impossible to live without failing at something, unless you live so cautiously, that you might as well not have lived at all – in which case you fail by default." — Anonymous

142. "Life doesn't require that we be the best, only that we try our best." – H. Jackson Brown Jr.

143. "The way I see it, every life is a pile of good things and bad things. The good things don't always soften the bad things, but vice versa, the bad things don't always spoil the good things and make them unimportant." –

144. "Life isn't about waiting for the storm to pass, it's about learning to dance in the rain." – Vivian Greene

145. "I enjoy life when things are happening. I don't care if it's good things or bad things. That means you're alive." – Joan Rivers

146. "There's more to life than basketball. The most important thing is your <u>family</u> and taking care of each other and loving each other no matter what." – Stephen Curry

147. "Today, you have 100% of your life left." – Tom

148. "Nobody who ever gave his best regretted it." – George Halas

149. "Make each day your masterpiece." – John Wooden

150. "You can't put a limit on anything. The more you dream, the farther you get." – Michael Phelps

151 "thinking positive is the key to success."-Rijo

Just reading to this thoughts is not enough you have apply this in your life
to became successful.

you just need to follow my steps to become successful in life.

you can write down changes you felt on the blank pages provided.

Steps

choose any 3 Quotes you can relate with.

write them down.

now it's your Dhamma to revise them atleast 10 times a day, at a intevel of atleast 1 hour.

After some time when your enegy will match the energy of the superior once you'll attrack success.